A Quick Guide to…

Gender Mainstreaming in Education

Elsa Leo-Rhynie and the
Institute of Development and Labour Law,
University of Cape Town, South Africa

Commonwealth Secretariat

Gender Management System Series

Commonwealth Secretariat
Marlborough House
Pall Mall, London SW1Y 5HX,
United Kingdom

© Commonwealth Secretariat,
June 1999

Designed and published by the
Commonwealth Secretariat.
Printed in the United Kingdom
by Abacus Direct.
Wherever possible, the
Commonwealth Secretariat uses
paper sourced from sustainable
forests or from sources that
minimise a destructive impact
on the environment.

Copies of this publication can
be ordered direct from:

Vale Packaging Ltd,
420 Vale Road, Tonbridge, Kent
TN9 1TD, United Kingdom
Tel: + 44 (0)1732 359387
Fax: +44 (0) 1732 770620
e-mail: vale@vale-ltd.co.uk

Price: £5.99
0-85092-599-1

Web sites:
http://www.thecommonwealth.org/gender
http://www.thecommonwealth.org
http://www.youngcommonwealth.org

Gender Management System Handbook

Using Gender-Sensitive Indicators: A Reference Manual for Governments and Other Stakeholders

Gender Mainstreaming in Development Planning: A Reference Manual for Governments and Other Stakeholders

Gender Mainstreaming in Finance: A Reference Manual for Governments and Other Stakeholders

Gender Mainstreaming in the Public Service: A Reference Manual for Governments and Other Stakeholders

Gender Mainstreaming in Education: A Reference Manual for Governments and Other Stakeholders

Gender Mainstreaming in Trade and Industry: A Reference Manual for Governments and Other Stakeholders

Gender Mainstreaming in Agriculture and Rural Development: A Reference Manual for Governments and Other Stakeholders

Gender Mainstreaming in Information and Communications: A Reference Manual for Governments and Other Stakeholders

Gender and Equal Employment Opportunities: A Reference Manual for Governments and Other Stakeholders

A Quick Guide to the Gender Management System

A Quick Guide to Using Gender-Sensitive Indicators

A Quick Guide to Gender Mainstreaming in Development Planning

A Quick Guide to Gender Mainstreaming in Finance

A Quick Guide to Gender Mainstreaming in the Public Service

A Quick Guide to Gender Mainstreaming in Education

A Quick Guide to Gender Mainstreaming in Trade and Industry

A Quick Guide to Gender Mainstreaming in Agriculture and Rural Development

A Quick Guide to Gender Mainstreaming in Information and Communications

A Quick Guide to Gender and Equal Employment Opportunities

Contents

Preface

In 1996, Commonwealth Ministers Responsible for Women's Affairs mandated the Commonwealth Secretariat to develop the concept of the Gender Management System (GMS), a comprehensive network of structures, mechanisms and processes for bringing a gender perspective to bear in the mainstream of all government policies, programmes and projects. The success of the GMS depends upon a broad-based partnership in society in which government consults and acts co-operatively with the other key stakeholders, who include civil society and the private sector. The establishment and strengthening of gender management systems and of national women's machineries was the first of 15 government action points identified in the 1995 Commonwealth Plan of Action on Gender and Development.

This *Quick Guide to Gender Mainstreaming in Education* has been produced to assist member governments in meeting their commitment to implementing the Plan of Action. It is an abridged version of the GMS publication *Gender Mainstreaming in Education: A Reference Manual for Governments and Other Stakeholders*, presenting the essential points of that document in an accessible way. It is hoped that both documents will be used by education policy-makers, personnel managers, planners, field staff and others, in conjunction with other GMS publications, including the Gender Management System Series, which provides tools and sector-specific guidelines for gender mainstreaming, including the *Gender Management System Handbook*.

The development of this guide and the Gender Management System Series has been a collaborative effort between the Commonwealth Secretariat's Gender and Youth Affairs Division and many individuals and groups. Their contribution to the thinking behind the GMS is gratefully acknowledged. In particular, I would like to thank the following: all those member governments who supported the development of the GMS and encouraged us to move the project forward; participants at the first GMS meeting in Britain in February 1997 and at the GMS Workshop in Malta in April 1998, who provided invaluable conceptual input and feedback; and the Steering Committee on the Plan of Action (SCOPA). I am also most grateful to: the various consultants who wrote and edited the text of the guide, including Professor Elsa Leo-Rhynie, University of the West Indies, research assistant Diana Thorburn, staff of the Institute of Development and Labour Law, University of Cape Town, and Daniel Woolford, Consultant Editor for the GMS publications; and the staff of the Gender Affairs Department, Gender and Youth Affairs Division, Commonwealth Secretariat, particularly Ms Eleni Stamiris, former Director of the Division, who took the lead in formulating the GMS concept and mobilising the various stakeholders in its development, Dr Judith May-Parker who provided substantive editorial input, and Dr Rawwida Baksh-Soodeen, Project Co-ordinator of the Gender Management System Series, who guided the project through to publication.

We hope that this resource series will be of genuine use to you in your efforts to mainstream gender.

Nancy Spence
Director
Gender and Youth Affairs Division
Commonwealth Secretariat

1 Introduction

Education, Gender and Development

Education is universally recognised as playing a key role in sustainable social and economic development. Regardless of the ideology underlying approaches to development, education is always cited as a priority area for attention and the investment of resources.

"The benefits of education are by now well established. Education improves the quality of life. It promotes health, expands access to paid employment, increases productivity in market and non-market work, and facilitates social and political participation."

Bellew and King, 1993: 285

That such benefits should be experienced by both women and men is fair and equitable. It is also increasingly recognised that ensuring that women receive education makes sense in terms of sustainable economic development. For example, the World Bank's 1996 progress report on the implementation of its gender policies indicated that since 1985, there had been increased lending for education programmes benefiting women, reflecting the Bank's recognition that educating women is one of the most important steps in promoting economic growth and development. The education of women is particular important given their reproductive role as homemakers and care-givers of children.

The education of girls and women is therefore an important investment, despite the precarious economic contexts within which many developing countries have to provide for education. Not only does education have a significant multiplier effect, given the responsibility of women for socialising the next generation, it also enhances the potential of women for contributing to the social, economic and political aspects of national development. Education also has considerable potential, in its many dimensions and processes, for bringing about change which can redress imbalances between women and men as well as other social groups.

However, considerable gender inequalities exist in the education sector. These inequalities are found not only in indicators which can be readily obtained from population census data, such as literacy, enrolment, achievement and levels of schooling attained, but also in several other aspects of education which are of concern in the pursuit of gender equality and equity, for example, management personnel in decision-making roles, curriculum content and reform, and teacher-student interaction.

Furthermore, current research on gender and education carried out internationally indicates that education, in its many facets of literacy, classroom interaction, curriculum, enrolment, attendance and achievement patterns, and teacher training, plays a significant role in perpetuating gender inequalities.

Gender, equality and equity

Gender refers to the socially constructed, rather than the biologically defined, sex roles and attributes of females and males. The 1995 Commonwealth Plan of Action on Gender and Development defines gender *inter alia*, as the socially defined/constructed differences between women and men that result in women's subordination and inequality in opportunity to a better life.

Gender refers to the historical and sociological relationships between women and men. If development is seen as an attempt to raise the quality of life of all people, gender in development works toward ensuring that the special needs of women vis-à-vis those of men, are met in this process. The approach presented in this guide recommends a process of gender analysis whereby differences in the status and experiences of women and men in education can be brought to light. In many cases, this may require specific measures to be taken so that women can enjoy the same rights, levels of achievement and standard of living that men do. The advantage of the gender approach is that it also brings to light situations in which it is men who are at a disadvantage – for example, the current under-achievement of young males in the educational systems of many Caribbean countries.

Although the terms gender equality and gender equity are often used interchangeably, they have come to have specific meanings. Gender equality refers to sameness or uniformity in quantity, amount, value and intensity of provisions made and measures implemented for women and men. Equality can usually be legislated. Gender equity refers to doing whatever is necessary to ensure equality of outcomes in the life experiences of women and men. Equity is difficult to legislate: identical treatment may satisfy the equality, but not the equity criterion.

Scope and Objectives of this Guide

The purpose of this guide is to provide guidelines for mainstreaming gender into the education sector, in particular the formal education sector (primary, secondary and tertiary education) of Ministries of Education.

The guide provides an overview of gender issues in the educational sector, including global and Commonwealth mandates for promoting gender equality. It examines such traditional indicators as literacy, enrolment, access to education and attainment, as well as other areas such as legal and administrative frameworks, the proportions of women in decision-making positions, resource allocation, curriculum development, and the organisation of schools and classrooms. It also examines ways in which gender inequalities are perpetuated through the education system.

The guide provides tools for gender analysis and proposes a number of policy interventions which governments may consider adopting, depending on particular national circumstances.

This guide is designed primarily for use by governments which are seeking to implement a policy of gender mainstreaming in their policies, plans and programmes. It is intended for use in the context of a Gender Management System, the gender mainstreaming model promoted by the Commonwealth to assist member countries in working towards gender equality and equity in government and in the broader civil society.

Gender Mainstreaming

Gender mainstreaming means the consistent use of a gender perspective at all stages of the development and implementation of policies, plans, programmes and projects. In the education sector, this would include not only the activities of governments, but also those of schools, colleges and education institutions, and, where appropriate, those of NGOs and the private sector as well.

Mainstreaming gender differs from previous efforts to integrate women's concerns into government activities in that, rather than 'adding on' a women's component to existing policies, plans, programmes and projects, a gender perspective informs these at all stages, and in every aspect of the decision-making process. Gender mainstreaming may thus entail a fundamental transformation of the underlying paradigms that inform education.

Why gender mainstreaming?

The concept of mainstreaming has developed out of a historical background of efforts to advance equality for women. In 1970, Ester Boserup used data and information on development projects in Third World countries to highlight the differential impact on women and men of development and modernisation strategies. Responding to this, liberal feminists in the United States advocated the use of legal and administrative reform to ensure that women and their concerns would be better integrated into economic systems. This led to the development of the Women in Development (WID) approach, based on the rationale that women constituted a large untapped resource which should be recognised as being potentially valuable in economic development.

The thinking behind the WID approach was strongly affected by the 'trickle down' and 'human capital' development theories of the 1960s and 1970s. These theories were based on the assumption that heavy investment in education systems and in the development of highly trained workers and managers would result in the transformation of 'backward', predominantly agricultural societies, into ones which were industrialised and modernised. The resultant improvements in living conditions, wages, health services, and education would then lead to a 'trickle down' effect in all sectors of the society, and it was assumed that women and men would benefit equally from these changes.

This assumption began to be questioned in the 1970s, however, as the relative position of women over the two decades of modernisation had not only shown very little improvement, but had actually declined in some sectors. In most countries, women's enrolment in educational institutions, particularly at secondary and tertiary levels, was not as high as men's. As new agricultural technologies were developed and introduced, their use was usually directed at men rather than women, despite the fact that many women were involved in agricultural production. And in the formal industrialised sector, women were usually found in low-skill, low-wage, repetitive jobs, which in some cases threatened their health. This was partly due to their low levels of education, but also to the belief that they were not the primary wage earners for their families. Gradually, it became widely recognised that women's experience of development was different from that of men, and research began to focus on women's views, opinions and experiences.

Initially, intervention programmes were designed using the women in development (WID) approach; providing services or introducing technologies which would reduce the workloads of women, so that they could participate more in educational and other opportunities offered by society. Very little work was done to try and determine why women had not benefited as much as men in the development process. There was an acceptance of the existing structures within society and an avoidance of any questioning of, or challenge to the origins of women's subordination. The WID approach also focused on sex as an analytical category without simultaneously examining the effects of race, class and culture; and the potential for, and actual discrimination and exploitation of women by women.

An alternative to the WID approach was offered in the 1980s: the gender and development (GAD) approach. This approach questioned the previous tendency to view women's problems in terms of their sex, i.e. their biological distinctions from men, rather than in terms of their gender, i.e. the social relationship between men and women in which women have been subordinated and oppressed. The GAD approach also emphasises the importance of taking into consideration class/caste and race/ethnic distinctions as these relate to gender. There is, however, the recognition that the concept of patriarchy – the process whereby societal power is generally invested in men, and the various structures of society consistently assign inferior and/or secondary roles to women – operates within as well as across classes/races to subordinate women.

The GAD approach supports the WID view that women should be given the opportunity to participate on equal terms in all aspects of life, but its primary focus is to examine the gender relations of power at all levels in society, so that interventions can bring about equality and equity between women and men in all spheres of life. The state is expected to assist in this process of promotion of women's emancipation, and has been called upon, for example, to assume the responsibility of facilitating women's participation in the productive sphere by providing social services such as child care, which women in many countries provide on a voluntary or private basis. The GAD approach also places strong emphasis on legal reform.

The WID approach is an 'add-on' rather than an integrative approach to the issue. In the GAD approach, women are viewed as agents of change rather than as passive recipients of development assistance. The intervention strategies of a GAD perspective do not seek merely to integrate women into ongoing developmental initiatives; they seek to bring about structural change and shifts in power relationships, and in so doing, to eliminate gender biases at all levels.

Mainstreaming gender in the education sector

Key issues and challenges involved in engendering the education sector incorporate both WID and GAD perspectives. These issues include:

✦ obtaining a clear quantitative picture of gender roles and ratios in various levels and areas of the educational system using sex-disaggregated data;

✦ identifying possible factors related to any gender gaps and inequalities identified, and planning for the elimination of these factors;

✦ assessing the educational needs, immediate and practical as well as long term and strategic, of girls and boys, women and men, and planning to meet these needs; and

✦ ensuring that women and men share equitably in the designing, planning, decision making, management, administration and delivery of education, and also benefit equitably in terms of access, participation and the allocation of resources.

Whereas a WID approach addresses some of women's needs, it does little to break down existing stereotypes and male-oriented cultural patterns. Most authorities have difficulty accepting gender as an important planning issue. This has been attributed to the fact that, although in many countries, women's bureaux and ministries have been established, the decision-making processes are still largely male-dominated and gender-blind. When gender planning does take place, it still tends to be an 'add-on' type of activity, and also perpetuates gender stereotypes (Moser, 1989).

It is important in planning policies and strategies for mainstreaming gender in the education system, therefore, to consider the theoretical bases from which development projects for women originate – the shift in emphasis from women in development to gender and development has the potential for more efficient use of development resources, and greater long term benefits, since a major objective of the GAD approach is ensuring that women are empowered to affect development planning and implementation.

The process of mainstreaming gender thus includes:
✦ questioning the underlying paradigm on which the national policy, goals and objectives have been based;
✦ joint programming with other development entities, including other government ministries and departments, intergovernmental and non-governmental organisations;
✦ aligning with other entities' priorities, activities and critical issues; placing gender-sensitive women and men in strategic positions in policy-setting and decision-making;
✦ making women visible in all data; and
✦ providing training in gender analysis, methodology and awareness.

These are important elements in the mainstreaming of gender in education, which will be guided by overall national goals, objectives and priorities, but should specifically seek to:
✦ make explicit the importance of gender along with race/ethnicity and social class/caste as a factor for consideration in the process of education;
✦ ensure gender equity in access both generally, and in relation to studies which lead to better careers and job opportunities;
✦ overcome structural barriers, whether they be legal, economic, political, or cultural which may influence the access and/or

participation of either sex in educational offerings;

✦ increase the awareness of the active role which women can and do play in development; and

✦ increase the participation of women in decision-making in the management and implementation of education.

2 Global and Commonwealth Mandates and Trends in the Education Sector

The mainstreaming of gender into all activities of government has received endorsement at the highest political levels. It is the central strategy of both the 1995 Commonwealth Plan of Action and the 1995 Beijing Declaration and Platform for Action. In addition, both these documents include specific references to the education sector.

Beijing and Education

The Fourth World Conference on Women in Beijing (1995) agreed on universal principles of gender equity and the Commonwealth member states are all signatories to the Beijing Declaration. Specific priorities of the Beijing Declaration are, *inter alia*, that:

✦ women's rights are human rights;

✦ women should have access to and enjoy the same standards of living as men;

✦ women have the right to freedom of thought, conscience, religion and belief, and the possibility of realising their own vision of their potential;

✦ women should participate in all levels of decision-making and have access to power;

✦ men and women should share family responsibilities equally, and women should be free to control all aspects of their health, especially their own fertility; and

✦ women should have access to economic resources, including land, credit, science and technology, vocational training, information, communication, markets, and of course, the world of learning: literacy, schooling and formal/informal education.

The Beijing Platform for Action includes a section on the education and training of women. The strategic objectives identified in that section are:

✦ ensure equal access to education;
✦ eradicate illiteracy among women;
✦ improve women's access to vocational training, science and technology, and continuing education;
✦ develop non-discriminatory education and training;
✦ allocate sufficient resources for and monitor the implementation of educational reforms;
✦ and promote lifelong education and training for girls and women.

Recognising that non-discriminatory education contributes to more equal relationships between men and women, the Platform for Action identifies areas in which discrimination in education exists, including:
✦ customary attitudes;
✦ early marriages and pregnancies;
✦ lack of gender awareness on the part of educators;
✦ girls' domestic responsibilities and the reduced time they are allowed for education;
✦ and sexual harassment.

Discrimination in education resources is found in:
✦ inadequate and gender-biased teaching and educational materials;
✦ lack of adequate schooling facilities, particularly for girls' special needs;
✦ stereotyped images of women and men in educational materials and teaching;
✦ gender-biased curricula and teaching materials which reinforce traditional sex roles;
✦ gender-biased science curricula and texts; and
✦ insufficient resources for education, particularly for females.

The Platform for Action recommends strategies specific to each of the above, and advocates use of other avenues for change, such as exploiting the potential of the powerful mass media as an educational tool, and specifically targeting the involvement of women in technology education.

Commonwealth Mandates

The 1995 Commonwealth Plan of Action on Gender and Development sets as a strategic objective of member governments to "take positive and/or affirmative action to provide equal opportunities in educational institutions...." To realise this and other strategic objectives, the Plan of Action proposed a number of action points that governments may wish to consider adopting, including action for human resource development – literacy, training and education, science and technology.

Specifically, the Plan of Action recommends the following actions:
+ undertake diverse and special training as well as informal and formal education programmes directed at women, including programmes to strengthen their self-esteem; and
+ encourage gender-inclusive curricula and devote particular attention to the participation of women in training-related programmes leading to occupations such as science and technology, industry and commerce.

The 1996 Commonwealth Women's Affairs Ministers' Meeting in Trinidad and Tobago reviewed progress in implementing the Plan of Action, and made further recommendations on its implementation. In particular, they recommended that Ministers of Education be requested to initiate more dynamic strategies for ensuring that women and girls are given equal access to educational opportunities, and participate more fully in training towards non-traditional occupations such as science, technology and commerce. They also recommended that additional resources be committed to distance education programmes such as those offered by the Commonwealth of Learning to help achieve these objectives.

A significant outcome of the meeting was the decision taken by Commonwealth Women's Affairs Ministers that member countries should be encouraged to achieve a target of at least 30 per cent women in decision-making in the political, public and private sectors by the year 2005. This proposal was endorsed by Commonwealth Heads of Government at their 1997 summit in Edinburgh.

Conferences of Commonwealth Education Ministers

Commonwealth Education Ministers, at their Thirteenth Conference in Botswana in 1997, commended the Secretariat for, among other activities, the pursuit of gender equity in its education work programme, and proposed that attention be given, *inter alia*, to continuing to address gender concerns in the educational system, paying attention to the problems of both girls and boys. They also commended such Commonwealth programmes as higher education activities targeting women managers.

The Twelfth Conference of Commonwealth Education Ministers, in Pakistan in 1994, called on member countries to make special efforts to enhance the participation of girls and women in science and technology (p. 9). It also called for a priority investment in women and girls as an initiative in human resource development (p. 23). Mention of lack of proper security for girls was listed as a reason for them being kept out of school (p. 30).

Education and Gender in the Commonwealth

Literacy and enrolment are the two main indicators cited in the gender and development literature with regard to education. These factors are essential to, but not sufficient for, the achievement of gender equality and equity in a society.

Literacy

Literate people are better able to control, manage and improve their health, nutrition and education. Where women are most often the carers of children, their literacy translates into increased competence in looking after their children. Further, advances in women's education and lower fertility rates are closely related.

Literacy is a basic tool for upward social mobility and an improved standard of living. A literate person not only has access to a wider range of jobs, and to better-paying jobs, but with the ability to read and write, a person can take advantage of continuing education. Educational qualifications are key to improving one's standard of living. In terms of empowerment, a literate person has greater access to sources of knowledge, and is better able to participate in decision-making in the family, community and wider society. In uplifting women's and men's lives, literacy is thus a fundamental priority. While literacy rates for both men and women have increased over the past 20 years, there are still many Commonwealth countries where women's literacy is considerably lower than men's (see Tables 1 and 2).

Enrolment

Enrolment in school is, like literacy, crucial to bettering one's life. Again, the figures for both sexes have increased in the past 30 years. Moreover, the differential between males' and females' enrolment is decreasing.

In some Commonwealth countries there are more females enrolled in school, at all levels, than males. Thus, while the quest for gender equality in education rightly focuses mainly on young women and girls, a case of reverse bias could be argued were the situation of boys and men not addressed too, particularly in those regions of the Commonwealth countries where enrolment, attendance and achievement rates are increasingly lower for boys than for girls. Of the 25 countries listed in Table 1, just over half, 13, have higher ratios for female secondary school enrolment, and 12 have higher, equal or practically equal ratios for female primary school enrolment (see Table 1).

Such data have been cited in support of the male marginalisation thesis as proposed by Miller (1994). The inference is that girls' successes are gained at the expense of boys' opportunities; but in most instances, the girls are outperforming boys despite the many obstacles, structural and cultural, which girls experience in gaining access to, and participating in educational activities. In Jamaica, for example, the number of places allocated to boys and girls in high schools result in many girls being denied places, despite the fact that their performance in the Common Entrance Examination for high schools is better than that of boys who are given places (Leo-Rhynie, 1996).

Other indicators

Ostergaard (1992), while acknowledging the importance of such indicators as literacy and enrolment, which provide data on the education stock, expresses the need for information on the 'flow of education'; indicators such as attendance, transition and retention rates, continuation data, areas of specialisation, and non-formal education.

Furthermore, in order to gain a full picture of gender imbalances and inequalities in the education sector, as well as on how such

Table 1   Educational Indicators for Selected Commonwealth Countries

Country	Adult Literacy Rate 1970		Adult Literacy Rate 1990		No. of Radio Sets per 1000 Pop. 1991
	f	m	f	m	
Australia	-	-	-	-	1268
Bangladesh	12	36	22	47	43
Botswana	44	37	65	84	122
Canada	-	-	-		1029
Ghana	18	43	51	70	268
India	20	47	34	62	79
Jamaica	97	96	99	98	420
Lesotho	74	49	-	-	32
Malawi	18	42	34	65	220
Malaysia	48	71	70	86	430
Mauritius	59	77	75	85	359
New Zealand	-	-	-		927
Namibia	-	-	-	-	127
Nigeria	14	35	40	62	173
Pakistan	11	30	21	47	90
Papua New Guinea	24	39	38	65	73
South Africa	-	-	75	78	303
Sierra Leone	8	18	11	31	223
Singapore	55	92	74	92	646
Sri Lanka	69	85	83	93	197
Tanzania	18	48	31	62	25
Trinidad and Tobago	89	95	93	96	492
Uganda	30	52	32	65	109
United Kingdom	-	-	-	-	1143
Zambia	37	66	65	81	81
Zimbabwe	47	63	60	74	84

Source: *The State of the World's Children 1995* (UNICEF, 1995)

o. of elevision ets Per 1000 op. 1991	Primary Enrolment Ratio (Gross) 1960		Primary Enrolment Ratio (Gross) 1986-92		Primary Enrolment Ratio (Net) 1986-92		% Primary School Children in Grade 5 1986-92	High School Enrolment Ratio (Gross) 1986-92	
	f	m	f	m	f	m		f	m
480	103	103	107	107	98	98	99	83	81
5	31	80	71	83	74	64	47	12	25
16	43	38	121	116	95	100	84	57	50
639	105	108	106	108	99	98	96	104	104
15	31	58	69	84	-	-	69	29	47
35	44	83	84	112	-	-	62	32	54
131	79	78	108	105	99	100	96	66	59
6	109	73	116	97	62	77	65	31	21
-	26	50	60	72	50	47	46	3	5
149	79	108	93	93	-	-	98	59	57
217	90	96	108	104	87	90	98	56	52
443	106	110	103	104	100	99	94	85	83
21	-	-	126	112	-	-	53	47	36
33	31	54	62	79	-	-	65	17	24
18	11	39	30	54	-	-	48	13	29
2	15	24	65	76	78	66	69	10	15
98	-	-	-	-	-	-	-	..	..
10	15	30	39	56	-	-	-	12	21
378	101	120	107	110	100	100	100	71	70
35	95	107	106	110	-	-	95	77	71
2	16	33	68	70	50	50	79	4	6
315	108	111	96	96	90	90	89	82	80
10	18	39	64	78	58	51	-	8	16
434	92	92	105	104	97	98	-	88	85
26	40	61	92	101	83	80	-	14	25
26	65	82	118	120	-	-	94	42	54

Table 2   Gender-Related Development Indicators for Selected
           Commonwealth Countries

Country	Life Expectancy at Birth (Years), 1994		Adult Literacy Rate (%), 1994		Combined Enrolment Ratio (%), 1994		Earned Income Share (%), 1994	
	f	m	f	m	f	m	f	m
Australia	81.0	75.2	99.0	99.0	80.0	77.0	39.8	60.2
The Bahamas	76.5	70.1	97.7	98.4	77.0	73.0	39.5	60.5
Bangladesh	56.5	56.3	24.3	48.4	34.0	45.0	23.1	76.9
Barbados	78.2	73.2	96.6	97.9	76.0	74.0	39.5	60.5
Botswana	53.7	50.5	58.0	79.3	72.0	70.0	38.9	61.1
Cameroon	56.5	53.7	49.5	74.0	42.0	51.0	30.9	69.1
Canada	81.7	76.3	99.0	99.0	100.0	100.0	37.8	62.2
Cyprus	79.2	74.9	94.0	94.0	75.0	75.0	27.1	72.9
Fiji Islands	74.1	69.9	89.2	93.7	78.0	80.0	21.4	78.6
The Gambia	47.2	44.0	22.7	50.9	27.0	41.0	37.8	62.2
Ghana	58.5	54.8	51.0	75.2	38.0	50.0	43.5	56.5
Guyana	66.7	60.0	97.4	98.5	67.0	66.0	26.4	73.6
India	61.4	61.1	36.1	64.5	47.0	63.0	25.7	74.3
Jamaica	76.1	71.7	88.4	79.6	67.0	64.0	39.2	60.8
Kenya	54.8	52.3	67.8	85.2	54.0	56.0	42.0	58.0
Lesotho	59.4	56.8	60.9	80.3	60.0	51.0	30.3	69.7
Maldives	61.5	64.2	92.9	93.1	70.0	70.0	35.4	64.6
Malta	78.6	74.1	86.0	86.0	75.0	79.0	20.9	79.1
Malawi	41.5	40.6	40.4	71.7	63.0	71.0	42.0	58.0
Malaysia	73.5	69.0	77.5	88.2	63.0	61.0	30.2	69.8
Mauritius	74.2	67.4	78.4	86.8	62.0	61.0	25.4	74.6
Mozambique	47.5	44.5	22.1	55.8	21.0	30.0	41.3	58.7
New Zealand	79.2	73.6	99.0	99.0	96.0	91.0	38.8	61.2
Nigeria	52.6	49.5	43.8	66.1	44.0	55.0	29.5	70.5
Pakistan	63.3	61.3	23.3	49.0	25.0	50.0	20.8	79.2
Papua New Guinea	57.3	55.8	60.7	79.8	34.0	41.0	34.8	65.2
South Africa	66.8	60.8	81.2	81.4	82.0	80.0	30.8	69.2
Sierra Leone	35.2	32.1	16.7	43.7	22.0	34.0	29.7	70.3

Country	Life Expectancy at Birth (Years), 1994		Adult Literacy Rate (%), 1994		Combined Enrolment Ratio (%), 1994		Earned Income Share (%), 1994	
	f	m	f	m	f	m	f	m
Singapore	79.3	74.9	87.2	95.6	71.0	73.0	30.7	69.3
Sri Lanka	74.6	70.0	86.9	93.2	68.0	65.0	34.5	65.5
Swaziland	60.5	56.0	73.3	76.4	70.0	74.0	34.9	65.1
Tanzania	51.7	48.9	54.3	78.8	33.0	35.0	47.3	52.7
Trinidad & Tobago	75.4	70.8	97.2	98.6	67.0	67.0	29.7	70.3
Uganda	41.1	39.3	48.7	73.2	30.0	39.0	40.7	59.3
United Kingdom	79.3	74.1	99.0	99.0	86.0	85.0	35.0	65.0
Zambia	43.3	41.7	69.3	84.4	44.0	51.0	38.8	61.2
Zimbabwe	50.1	48.1	79.0	90.2	64.0	72.0	37.4	62.2

Source: *Human Development Report 1995* (UNDP, 1995)

inequalities are perpetuated through education, it is necessary to focus on such indicators as:

+ management structures (i.e. female/male representation in decision-making at Ministry, School Board and institutional levels);
+ access (e.g. male/female admissions at different levels);
+ resource allocation (e.g. per capita expenditure on female and male students);
+ achievement (i.e. female/male performance in national examinations).

These are examined in greater detail in Section 5.

3 Gender in the Education Sector

Gender inequalities and inequities are both manifested in the education sector and perpetuated through educational structures and processes. A number of issues have been identified which bear upon existing inequalities and their perpetuation within the education system. In examining these issues, it should be borne in mind that they are general trends rather than fixed norms. The situation varies from country to country and, even within one country, is constantly evolving.

Gender Role Socialisation

Various theories have been proposed to explain the complex process of gender role socialisation. It is generally agreed that gender role socialisation begins in the family, and that nursery and primary schools continue the process as well as play a part in constructing gender through their organisation and practices. These processes and practices are then continued by the secondary and tertiary education system, though perhaps in different ways, as children progress into adolescence and then adulthood. The media, interaction with other children and other factors also contribute to the gender socialisation process (Measor and Sikes, 1992: 50).

The post-modern feminist discourse emphasises difference across race/ethnicity, class/caste and culture lines, and thus highlights the importance of gender analysis, and policies and programmes which are sensitive to social and cultural norms. Recognition of the importance of this sensitivity makes it very difficult to develop 'generic' gender analytic tools for use in a variety of countries. No single perspective is able to represent the variety and breadth of issues in gender and education. Together, however, and informed by other perspectives, these approaches can help build a comprehensive picture of the multi-dimensional education process and its role in gender inequity. Any analysis or attempt to mainstream gender must employ a holistic approach, examining institutions and practices in depth.

School Organisation

The issue of coeducational versus single-sex schools has been the topic of some research. The findings are mixed, with some researchers reporting that the sex composition of the school makes very little difference to the achievement of female and male students, while others note significantly higher achievement for both sexes in single sex schools. One recommendation is that for certain subjects, the best method of achieving equity is to teach the sexes separately, even though the school may be coeducational.

However, it is also argued that the splitting of pupils into groups on the basis of sex is usually justified not on educational grounds, but for reasons of organisational convenience, and that the convenience of sex-segregation is outweighed by the disadvantageous side-effect that it reinforces taken-for-granted views of 'innate' gender differences in interests and abilities. It is argued that sex segregation in school may reduce the opportunities pupils have to test gender stereotypes against the actual behaviour of classmates of the other sex. On this view, the significance of sex-segregation in schools should not be underestimated because the few situations in which girls and boys are treated differently may assume a special importance with respect to evolving definitions of femininity and masculinity.

General Content and Structure of Schooling

The view that schools transmit our 'common cultural heritage' has given way to a recognition that out of the enormous range of ideas, values and knowledge available in any culture, only a fraction is selected as suitable for transmission in schools. The question is: what are the criteria behind this selection, which social groups benefit from the inclusion of their forms of thought, and which social groups lose through the exclusion of their forms of thought?

There are persistent sex differences in educational processes within the schools, based on cultural beliefs about sex differences between women and men in both character and ability. Females and males are subjected to differential socialisation in mixed classrooms and are rewarded for different things. Females tend to learn 'femininity' instead of 'masculinity', i.e. they learn to be docile and subservient instead of independent and thoughtful.

Young women and men get very different kinds of preparation for work. At the secondary level, in job-training and in post-secondary education, young women and men 'choose' courses that are predominantly filled with one sex or the other. Thus they enter the labour market with different skills and interests that lead to differential treatment by employers.

What is reproduced in school is a gendered society. What we want young people to learn in school is shaped by gender relations and by notions of what young men and women will do differently at work.

The distinction between women's knowledge and men's knowledge is deeply ingrained in the curriculum. Women's knowledge has been vocational, designed for the practicalities of being a woman, designed for the private sphere. The rest of the curriculum has been designed to educate men for the public sphere. Both the content and the structure of schooling and training have been designed to prepare young people for a male world. School has traditionally been a preparation for the public, productive sphere, ignoring the private sphere. Learning for family and personal life has been relegated to the family.

Curriculum

The curriculum, from pre-primary to tertiary level, has been subjected to analysis, and gender biases have been identified in the teaching objectives, the subject choices offered, and the teaching materials. Very often the persons developing, as well as those delivering the curriculum, are unaware of these biases and so the blatant as well as the subtle distinctions and discriminations persist.

Differentiated learning pervades the curriculum. There is a widespread built-in assumption that practical subjects for girls should relate to their future roles as mothers and home-makers, while boys are more likely to need preparation for entry into the world of formal employment, and curricular arrangements such as scheduling allow these differences to persist. Most areas of study exclude or trivialise women's contributions, experiences or knowledge. Frequently, different subjects are provided for girls and boys.

These differences can be maintained through tradition and custom. For instance, since adolescent girls may avoid maths and science courses and have lower achievement scores in these areas, they may be less prepared to enter the academic high schools once reserved for men. Girls are also less often exposed to mechanics courses, which would prepare them to enter traditionally male, vocational, high schools. Some countries are addressing this problem by ensuring that both girls and boys are exposed to such classes as design and information technology as well as cookery/domestic science.

Even the teaching of the same subjects can have the effect of reproducing gender divisions. There are two ways in which teachers tend to perpetuate gender divisions between girls and boys in their classroom.

First, research on the way teachers divide their energies among their pupils has shown that there may be an unintended consequence of disadvantaging girls. Teachers tend to focus more attention on boys than on girls in their classroom. This has some important consequences:

1 Female students are less likely to be challenged and stretched academically, with serious implications for their future performance.
2 Because they are less likely than boys to be singled out as worthy recipients of the teacher's attention, girls feel less valued in the classroom, reinforcing other pressures that urge them to take a back seat in classroom activity.
3 This may in turn affect their confidence regarding speaking publicly, and thus their participation in politics and the public sphere.

Teachers should make a conscious effort to channel more of their attention and energies to quieter pupils. The neglect of quiet pupils in the classroom works, on the whole, to the disadvantage of girls. It is only when teachers create an atmosphere in which girls and boys are, and know themselves to be, equally valued and equally welcome, that girls will be positively encouraged to voice their opinions and ideas. There is evidence, moreover, that a teacher's encouragement is important to the student's career decision.

Secondly, the style of teaching in mixed classes may incline pupils to believe that the subject is more appropriate for one sex than the other. Curriculum reform will require a fundamental reworking of what knowledge is valued in the curriculum, how that knowledge is made available and how it is taught.

Educational Materials

Much research has been conducted on this topic, and the implications have been noted of the intensive and extensive use of texts in which the stereotyping of gender roles is explicit. Sex stereotypes in society are reflected in inequities in curricular materials, which usually portray females and males differently. Textbooks and tests often depict women and men in traditional roles and occupations that are even more sex-segregated than those they actually fill.

As regards textbooks, research has indicated that there are no sex differences in the kinds of environment in which female and male children are portrayed, but there are differences in the environments portrayed of adults:

+ Adult females are much more often portrayed in the home, and adult males are more often seen outdoors, in business, and at school. Social studies, literature and history syllabuses fail to give full due to the range of activity of both sexes, and incorporate values and assumptions that downgrade and devalue women's experience and achievement.
+ As regards illustrations in textbooks, white males are overly represented and shown in a much wider range of occupations than females.
+ The research also indicated that in test materials, as with textbooks, there was a vast over-representation of content related to males.

The adverse effect of sex-stereotyped educational materials on children's occupational aspirations may be assumed. Thus the production of texts which provide alternatives to those in use, and the training of teacher educators so that they can develop and share a critical perspective even when they are forced to use such texts, is vitally important.

Perceptions and Attitudes

Gender inequalities in the education sector are perpetuated by the perceptions and attitudes of a number of different stakeholders.

Girls' own perceptions

Young women may be unwilling to deviate from sex-role norms during adolescence or to take classes judged inappropriate for them because of peer pressures and the attitudes of male classmates. Furthermore, income differences between women and men, inadequate provision of public child-care facilities and the predominance of families with a traditional division of labour are all part of the world young girls know. Their experience takes on meanings that lead to an expectation that traditional patterns will be continued. Elements of domestic gender relations and norms still shape the way they see acceptable options. Any attempt to show young girls that the world is constructed in a way that might be changed, involves not just talking to them, but also showing them that conditions can indeed be altered. Therefore, political movements need to push for institutional change that demonstrates the possibility of change in the broader society.

There is also the problem of girls' lack of career planning. The more definitely girls plan their working careers, the more their occupational choices will resemble those of men. Planning for a continuous attachment to the labour force will move women in the direction of men's jobs. Young women's changed responses would change the context in which young men have to act. Being confronted with young women who expect equal relationships or no relationships will produce a changed set of rewards and sanctions for male behaviour, thus requiring young men to accept young women as their equals.

Parental attitudes

Parents' lack of awareness about the benefits of education and training girls for girls plays a role in perpetuating gender inequalities. Research has indicated that there is an inter-generational transmission of behaviours and attitudes. Therefore, it is important for parents to develop a positive attitude towards education for their daughters.

Career counselling

Career counsellors have tended to hold traditional attitudes about appropriate occupations for female and male students, discouraging non-traditional aspirations and channelling women into sex-typical occupational choices.

Employers' attitudes

The relationship between education and the labour market requires careful attention. It would not help women to diversify their education and training if no one would employ them once they were qualified. Employers' attitudes often result in discouraging job prospects for young educated women.

When asked for an explanation for employment patterns, employers cited poor education in inappropriate subjects. This, they thought, was possibly the result of poor career advice. Traditionally, only a small number of women have been educated in scientific or industry-oriented subjects, affecting employers' perceptions of their suitability for training. This is important because employers do not offer only jobs but opportunities for on-the-job training. Those with approved backgrounds are therefore higher up in the queue for recruitment. Employers' preconceptions of women make them treat women (as a group) as a poor investment and this will be reflected in recruitment. Women face discrimination in certain professions because it is expected that they may become pregnant or have children to care for.

Sex-Based Harassment

This area of research is fairly recent but is yielding much information which previously had remained hidden. The research points to the abuse which many female students suffer as members of mixed sex classes, and the lack of sanctions applied to male students and even in some cases male teachers who are guilty of this behaviour. The harassment of young female teachers by male students has also been documented.

Sex-based harassment, which can include a range of behaviours, is based on the presumption of power relations which discriminate against girls and women. Sex-based harassment relegates girls and women to an inferior position relative to boys and men, and makes a female feel embarrassed, frightened, hurt or uncomfortable because of her sex. The impact on the social and educational experience of girls can be devastating. In some cases girls escape either by ceasing to attend particular subjects or by leaving the school altogether.

Girls at Risk

Another problem relates to girls who are at risk. These include pregnant teenagers or teenage mothers, girls assisting their mothers with domestic tasks, girls suffering from domestic violence or physical or sexual abuse, girls suffering from serious health problems and homeless girls. Girls at risk experience school-related problems because the curriculum, teaching practice and organisation of schools do not meet their needs. These girls get lower grades and may passively or even actively opt out of schooling.

Vocational Training

Vocational education programmes have traditionally been sex-segregated, channelling males and females into different courses. While females are trained predominantly in health, home economics, and office and business programmes, males can be found primarily in technical preparation, the trades and agriculture. Enrolment in such programmes has a significant impact on subsequent employment. Women are also under-represented in apprenticeships because they are less likely to learn about programmes, to qualify, and to be selected. The third and most important source of training occurs on the job. Female jobs are less likely than male jobs to provide on-the-job training.

Informal Interaction Among Students

Although this takes place on a continual basis it is very often facilitated through clubs and societies, sport and other out of classroom activities. Many of these clubs are single-sex, for example Boy Scouts and Girl Guides, so leadership opportunities exist for both male and female students – although they do tend to occur in the context of gender-stereotyped activities. Where clubs are mixed, it is often the case that leadership is dominated by one sex and the club is often seen as being a 'male' club, (e.g. the science club) or a 'female' club, (e.g. the cookery club). The 'gender' of the club is usually perceived in stereotypical terms.

4 Strategies and Processes for Mainstreaming Gender in the Education Sector

The Gender Management System

To assist member governments in mainstreaming gender into their activities, the Commonwealth is promoting the Gender Management System (GMS), an integrated network of structures, mechanisms and processes designed to make government more gender-aware, increase the numbers of women in decision-making roles within and outside government, facilitate the formulation of gender-sensitive policies, plans and programmes, and promote the advancement of gender equality and equity in the broader civil society.

The enabling environment of a GMS

The establishment and operation of a Gender Management System requires an enabling environment. There are a number of interrelated factors that determine the degree to which the environment in which the GMS is being set up does or does not enable effective gender mainstreaming. These determining factors of the enabling environment include the following:

+ political will and commitment to gender equality at the highest levels;
+ global and regional mandates such as the Commonwealth Plan of Action, the Beijing Platform for Action and Convention on the Elimination of all Forms of Discrimination Against Women (CEDAW);
+ a legislative and constitutional framework that is conducive to advancing gender equality;
+ the presence of a critical mass of women in decision-making roles;
+ an autonomous civil society and the role it can play in advancing gender equality;
+ adequate human and financial resources; and
+ donor aid and technical assistance, such as that provided by multilateral and bilateral agencies.

GMS structures and functions

The structural and functional elements of the GMS can be summarised as follows:

✦ a Lead Agency (usually the Ministry of Women's/Gender Affairs or other National Women's Machinery), which initiates and strengthens the GMS institutional arrangements, provides overall co-ordination and monitoring, and carries out advocacy, communications, media relations and reporting;

✦ a GMS Management Team (consisting of representatives from the Lead Agency, core government ministries such as Finance, Development Planning, Public Service, and Legal Affairs, and a representative of civil society), which provides leadership for the implementation of the GMS, defines broad operational policies, indicators of effectiveness, and timeframes for implementation;

✦ Gender Focal Points (senior staff in core and sectoral ministries), which co-ordinate gender activities (e.g. training), promote gender mainstreaming in all activities in their respective sectors, and sit on the Inter-Ministerial Steering Committee (see below);

✦ an Inter-Ministerial Steering Committee (whose members are representatives of the Lead Agency and the Gender Focal Points all ministries), which ensures that gender mainstreaming in government policy, planning and programmes in all sectors is co-ordinated and that strong linkages are established between ministries;

✦ a Parliamentary Gender Caucus (consisting of women and gender-aware male parliamentarians), which carries out awareness raising, lobbying, and promoting the participation of women in politics; and

✦ representatives of civil society (Gender Equality Commission/Council, academic institutions, NGOs/professional associations, media, the private sector and other stakeholders), who provide inputs to gender analysis, policy and planning, and monitoring and evaluation.

GMS processes

The processes involved in implementing a Gender Management System include developing and implementing a national Gender Action Plan, which should include provisions for setting up or strengthening the GMS structures and mechanisms, and for engendering core ministries and sectoral policy and planning. Normally spearheaded by the Ministry of Women's/Gender Affairs or other national women's machinery, the Gender Action Plan should include specific guidelines for setting up Gender Focal Points and mainstreaming gender into the regular policy, planning and implementation cycles of the Ministry of Education. These cycles have five main phases, and a gender perspective needs to be integrated in each phase:

1 Gender analysis: this involves analysing the status of women vis-à-vis men in the sector and examining the impact on women and men of education policy.

2 Policy development and appraisal: establishing gender priorities according to individual national circumstances, developing policy options to address gender imbalances, and appraising options to determine their gender impact.

3 Gender-aware action plans: the output of policy development is a plan which should have a clearly defined gender dimension.

4 Implementation: the implementation of the engendered work plan takes place as part of the normal functioning of government.

5 Monitoring and evaluation: this involves reviewing key indicators on the status of women in the national context in the education sector, and feeding the findings into the next planning cycle.

Prioritising Goals

The prioritisation of goals and areas for action in mainstreaming gender depends to a large extent on the source of the expressed need for change and the triggers for this change. In most instances, mainstreaming is initiated through a policy statement. Such policy statements usually emanate from a development plan or strategy that has benefited from gender-sensitive intervention – by non-governmental organisations, development agencies, women's organisations and/or women and men who have convinced the government of the advantages, and indeed the necessity for such change.

In some instances, the change is triggered by the requirements of international agencies that insist on countries meeting certain conditions relating to gender equity, and make these conditions a prerequisite for the granting of financial assistance. In such a 'top-down' scenario, the institutional environment may be required to implement change advocated by policy directives, and institutions may respond differently to these requirements. Responses can range from enthusiasm to a cautious acceptance and a willingness to comply, or even to strong resistance.

Sometimes the call for change comes from within individual institutions (a 'bottom-up approach' to mainstreaming). The process here could involve a group of teachers and/or students identifying the need for change in a variety of areas, and working towards effecting this change. In such a situation, changes at the classroom, staff room and local institutional level, such as in access, participation, resource allocation and achievement of male and female students may precede and trigger mainstreaming in institutional management and the policy environment.

The objectives of such localised action are usually targeted at bringing about change within the institutional environment and possibly also working towards having this recognised as a model for change in other institutions. The often quasi-subversive action involved in bringing about such change is usually highly motivated, and can greatly facilitate a national thrust towards gender equality if the persons initiating the change are co-opted to be members of the institutional arrangements for gender mainstreaming, such as a Gender Management System. The ultimate goal is to influence policy as it relates to a large number of institutions, and a local success story can contribute to the framing of such a policy and its recommendations.

Legislative change, for example in the form of a Code of Regulations establishing a framework around which other changes can be developed, may come first; or changes in attitudes brought about by increased awareness of gender issues may result in calls for, and the implementation of, legislative change.

Gender Awareness Training

Gender mainstreaming may necessitate the provision of significant educational input in the form of gender awareness training, geared towards changing established cultural norms of behaviour and obtaining acceptance of new and different goals and objectives. Such training should be developed around hard data – both quantitative and qualitative – from which training needs may be ascertained, and must be conducted at different levels.

This training should be designed to achieve the following goals:
+ assist staff in developing alternative perspectives on gender issues;
+ build capacity in gender analysis;
+ ensure that a gender perspective is included in the policy-setting and decision-making processes; and
+ permit the framing of appropriate policy guidelines and directives to advance gender equality.

Gender awareness training should also reach beyond government institutions to involve all stakeholders – teachers, parents, students (particularly in tertiary level institutions), places of worship and religious organisations (where these are sponsors of schools), and non-governmental organisations and community groups who have a strong influence on the opinions, attitudes and behaviours of persons in small communities.

Involving Other Stakeholders

Whether the triggers for mainstreaming are 'top-down' or 'bottom-up', the involvement of all the key stakeholders in the system is crucial. The commitment of those who are part of the process, and/or who are influential in the implementation of the process, is essential if success is to be realised. In the setting of policy, a broad consultative group which includes all stakeholders will ensure their involvement, and hopefully also their agreement and commitment to the demands of the policy agreement. Stakeholders should be part of the membership of both the National and Institutional Consultative Committees in order to facilitate their involvement in the implementation process. It is only when this is assured that the implementation process can be fully examined and the priority areas for action decided upon. The stakeholders very often also provide some of the resources necessary for the full implementation and so their 'buy-in' to the process becomes vital.

In the bottom-up scenario, the stakeholders' concurrence with the change will also be crucial if it is to be moved from the local to the institutional and policy levels. Initiators of the change in this case, therefore, will have to lobby the stakeholders, individually or collectively, and work towards gaining their support.

5 Guidelines for Conducting a Gender Impact Analysis

Countries differ tremendously in levels of development, in degree of gender asymmetry, and in cultural and traditional attitudes to gender. Moreover, gender intersects with social class/caste, race/ethnicity, culture/religion and age as a basis for inequity, subordination and discrimination in access to opportunity, and all of these factors are manifested differently in different countries. Measuring gender inequity and prescribing for gender equity is thus a highly complex and country-specific, as well as a fluid and dynamic process.

The first step is to gather relevant data on education. As mentioned previously, enrolment, literacy and even achievement statistics cannot reveal the entire picture. In developed countries, for example, where data show gender equality in education, there may still exist textbooks and/or curricula which portray gender stereotypes and which influence girl students to choose less self sufficient career paths, thus increasing the likelihood of their dependency on men. Another possibility is that the content and methodology of science subjects may be biased toward male students and their learning patterns. Measuring variables such as these should take place on a local as well as a national level, and is important in planning interventions to bring about change.

Gender Analysis Frameworks

Three major gender planning/analytical frameworks are noted in the literature on gender and development:
+ The Harvard Framework, developed by Overholt *et al* (1985), concentrates primarily on gathering gender-disaggregated data, so as to have a clear quantitative picture of gender roles and ratios. Other quantitative data, such as age, resources, benefits and time spent on activities are also important in the construction of this picture. This method also identifies

possible factors relating to gender asymmetries and analyses these in relation to the data.

✦ The Moser Method, based on Molyneux (1985) and Moser (1989), builds on the concepts of practical and strategic gender needs. Practical needs refer to women's immediate needs, 'special' needs that are often overlooked by development planners and policy-makers. Examples are provision of child care facilities, or introduction of technology to alleviate onerous domestic chores. Strategic needs are those which are more concerned with long term emancipation and empowerment for women, and may not directly affect or involve women in need. Examples are legal provisions designed to achieve gender equality. To these concepts is added the tool of classifying women's activities into three main groups: reproductive work, productive work and community managing activities. Distinguishing what women do in each of these roles, what they need to deal better with these roles, and what could possibly be done in the long term to restructure these roles so they are more equitably shared with men, comprises the basis of this method.

✦ The Women's Empowerment Framework, described by Longwe and Clarke (1994), can be linked to the DAWN (Development Alternatives with Women for a New Era) network, which advocates women's participation and control in decision-making and development planning. Women's ability and freedom to control their lives, and to have a say in the changes to their world, are tantamount to women's empowerment and equity with men. This may be described as a grassroots approach in that it seeks to have women whose lives are to be affected by development policies participate directly in the formulation and decision-making of these policies. This involves sensitisation of women, and mobilisation of women to participate at all levels of decision-making.

Each method focuses on different indicators of gender inequity/inequity, and prescribes different measures for action toward change. They all have their advantages.

These guidelines propose the use of indicators which reflect an acceptance of the value of aspects of all three frameworks. The indicators are classified into three main categories:

✦ the policy environment;
✦ the institutional environment; and
✦ the critical policy indicators.

A series of questionnaire templates for obtaining data using these indicators is provided in the Appendix of the full-length version of this guide, *Mainstreaming Gender in Education: A Reference Manual for Governments and Other Stakeholders*.

The Policy Environment

These indicators will assess the adequacy of the statement of policy as it relates to gender, the involvement of institutions which could provide technical assistance in the framing of the policy, the gender composition of management, as well as the legal and other mechanisms in place to support the policy in its implementation and review.

The policy environment reflects the extent to which the policy-making/executive level management of the country's educational system is ready to integrate gender into its goals, objectives, plans, programmes, projects and activities. This readiness is demonstrated in the gender balance of the power structure and policy-making bodies of the Ministry of Education, School Boards, and the gender representation in decision-making. It is clearly indicated in policy documents/statements and practices that explicitly acknowledge and reflect issues relating to gender; for example, in the Code of Regulations, in promotional opportunities, and in compensation.

Gender analysis of an education system requires the involvement, at the levels of policy-making, management and administration, of women and gender-aware men who are sensitive to practical as well as strategic gender needs, and who can take an active role in trying to meet these needs. Legislation is a powerful tool in the achievement of this objective.

Indicators relating to the policy environment are:

Clarity and suitability of the policy statement with regard to gender

✦ **The policy statement:** Is there a stated policy related to gender? To what extent is the stated policy an effective tool in terms of guiding the goals, plans and activities at all levels of the educational system as they relate to gender? Does it identify critical indicators?

✦ **The policy review:** How effective are the mechanisms for effecting the above and for reviewing the policy, as well as changing it if and when necessary? Is the policy stated for a specific time period or is its life indefinite?

✦ **Implementation problems:** What are the problems presented by the policy, and what are the barriers to the full implementation of the policy as stated?

The nature of management/decision-making

✦ **Composition of management:** What is the gender composition of the Ministry of Education hierarchy; the gender composition of School Boards; reporting relationships and the power structure?

✦ **Representation in decision-making:** What is the female/male representation in decision-making at the Ministry of Education and on School Boards?

✦ **Code of Regulations:** Does a Code of Regulations exist to guide the management and operations of schools? Does this Code reflect the gender policy of the Ministry of Education?

✦ **Compensation:** What are the female/male differentials in salaries and benefits at different age levels?

✦ **Promotional opportunities:** What are the female/male differentials in appointments at Education Officer, Senior Education Officer, Chief Education Officer, at different age levels?

✦ **Challenges to power:** What formal mechanisms exist to challenge the management e.g. trade unions? Is gender one of the issues which is a priority? What informal mechanisms are used to challenge management, e.g. demonstrations, lobby, petitions etc.?

✦ **Institutional autonomy:** How much effective autonomy can individual institutions exercise? Who recruits, rewards, disciplines and manages staff? What are the female/male differentials in appointments at Senior Teacher/Head of Department/Vice Principal/Principal level, at different age levels? Does a system of mentoring and succession sequence planning exist? To what extent is such a plan gender-sensitive? What problems does the level of autonomy allowed each institution create in terms of monitoring gender policy?

The Institutional Environment

The implementation of an education policy which has gender objectives requires an institutional environment which is sensitive and receptive to meeting the special needs of girls and boys. The institutional environment reflects the extent to which an individual institution is aware of, and ready to, implement programmes and practices to address gender issues and promote gender equity. This readiness is demonstrated by the gender composition of School Boards, the gender composition of staff, their working conditions, and the development and implementation of specific policies such as those relating to subject choices available to female and male students, and sexual harassment.

Examination of these indicators will involve the collection of sex-disaggregated data to obtain a clear quantitative picture of the roles which women and men play in the institution, and the provisions made and resources allocated to meet the specific needs of female and male students. Internal and external perceptions of gender equity at the institution are also explored.

The indicators relating to the institutional environment are:

Representation in decision-making: What is the female/male institutional representation on the management team or School Board? Is the representation indicative of the female/male staff composition (e.g. if the staff is 80 % female, and two staff representatives sit on the Board, are they both male)?

Staff: What proportion of men/women are represented in the academic/teaching cadre; in the administrative/secretarial staff; in the ancillary staff? Are men/women on the teaching staff equally qualified? Do women teach subjects which are stereotypically female, e.g. language, and men those stereotypically male, e.g. science?

Working conditions: What are the problems faced in attracting and retaining qualified men/women? What constraints and problems do men/women face?

Sexual harassment: Does a policy exist? Does the policy address intimidation and such harassment as may occur within the learning environment between female and male students? What is the incidence, and is there an accepted strategy for dealing with any incident of sexual harassment; at the local level; at the Ministry of Education level?

Internal and external perceptions: Is the institution perceived to be one which is gender-fair by persons working in the institution; by persons external to the institution?

Critical Policy Indicators

These indicators provide detailed data which can point to and guide the nature of interventions which need to be made in order to effect meaningful change. They assess gender differentials in provision, access, allocation of resources, participation and achievement/impact within the educational system. The critical policy indicators are:

Nature of the educational provision

Level: What is the provision made for school places at primary, secondary and tertiary levels, and are there any differences related to gender?

Availability: Is education equally available to female and male students, e.g. if there are single sex schools, do more exist for boys than for girls or vice versa?

Access

Access: Is there open access to female and male students at primary, secondary, tertiary levels? Does this result in equal representation of female/male students at each level? Is there any conflict between policy and cultural practices with regard to taking advantage of access, and participation by female/male students?

Eligibility criteria: Do entry requirements/qualifications discriminate against female or male students? Are there different provisions made for female/male students which would facilitate one over the other?

Participation

Enrolment: What are the female/male differences in enrolment at primary, secondary, tertiary levels? Is there any conflict between policy and cultural practices with regard to enrolment and participation of male/female students?

Attendance: What are the female/male differences in attendance at primary, secondary, tertiary levels? Is there any conflict between policy and cultural practices with regard to attendance and participation of female/male students?

Legislation: Is attendance compulsory; for girls and boys; at what levels? Is compulsory attendance monitored equally for female and male students?

Curriculum: Who was involved in formulating the curriculum? Do the aims and content of the curriculum reflect gender biases? Do textbooks and other teaching materials portray traditional female/male stereotypes? Is there differential male/female participation in subjects/courses/programmes at secondary and tertiary levels? What is the relationship of subjects being pursued by female and male students to the gender division of labour, and occupational gender stereotyping? Is there a state/school policy re: subject offerings to female/male students?

Learning environment: Are teachers aware of gender issues and concerns, and do they make an effort to provide equal attention to female and male students, to avoid sexist and discriminatory comments, examples and behaviour in their classrooms? Do teachers use a variety of teaching styles, or do they concentrate on those which are more suited to the learning styles of female/male students?

Co-curricular activities: Is there equal provision for co-curricular activities of female/male students? Are there gender-exclusive co-curricular activities, e.g. sports, clubs, societies? What is the female/male composition of the management and membership of student-run clubs, societies?

Student promotion: Are there policies governing the mechanism for student promotion – from primary to secondary; from secondary to tertiary; as well as within the primary and secondary systems? Are these in any way gender discriminatory, in statement or in practice?

Dropout/continuation: What are the dropout rates at primary, secondary and tertiary levels of female/male students? If there is a gender differential in dropout rates, what are the factors related to this? Are these factors the same at primary, secondary and tertiary levels? What is the female/male graduation rate from secondary school?

Resources

Teaching staff: Have teachers received any training in gender studies? Do the curricula of teacher education programmes reflect the importance of this issue in the preparation of teachers for work in schools?

Cost: What is the nature of the financial support provided for schools? Government supported, cost sharing, private funds? Are there any differences related to gender? What is the average cost per female/male student at primary, secondary, tertiary levels?

Decision-making regarding resource use: How is resource use determined? Does the mechanism in place present problems for monitoring gender policy?

Achievement/Impact

Literacy: What are the levels of literacy for women and for men?

Achievement at primary, secondary, tertiary levels: What are the female/male differentials in terms of entry for and success in achievement tests at primary, secondary and tertiary levels?

Specific subject/course/programme achievement: Is female/male achievement at secondary and tertiary levels similar in specific subject areas and in specific courses and programmes? What is the relationship of the subjects, courses, programmes pursued to the division of labour along gender lines?

Development of specific social attitudes and values: To what extent are there female/male differences in the development of social attitudes and values expressed through a broad socio-economic, political and cultural understanding of society; a commitment to changing inequitable yet traditionally inscribed female/male roles; activities such as leadership in educational institutions as well as in community settings; and skills such as articulateness in public/formal settings?

Placement of female/male graduates: How readily do graduates find employment? Are female/male graduates with similar qualifications employed at similar levels and with similar salaries and benefits?

6 Policy Interventions

Gender Analysis of the Data

The data obtained using the critical policy indicators will provide both quantitative and qualitative information that is crucial in the development of a gender-sensitive educational policy, and must be considered together in the formulation of policy recommendations and operational objectives. Figure 1 provides a simple example.

The need for flexibility

Countries vary widely in terms of educational indicators as well as cultural, social and economic specifics. These guidelines are intended, not to provide blanket generalisations covering this wide diversity, but rather to be adapted and prioritised according to countries' specific national circumstances.

The process of interpreting the data and translating it into practical techniques for prioritising areas for policy intervention must therefore be responsive to local cultural norms and practices, and must meet the needs of the people in that setting. The guidelines that should be selected and utilised are those that are particularly suited to the individual country situation. Important considerations in this regard are:
+ the needs in the particular setting;
+ priority considerations, given the triggers for change;
+ the extent of the willingness to change; and
+ resources available to effect the change.

The data generated from the research on critical policy indicators must be relied upon to guide priorities in specific settings. In Figure 2, an example demonstrates the difference which a knowledge and understanding of the particular setting makes in the interpretation of quantitative data. The example also underlines the importance of obtaining qualitative information as a supplement to quantitative data.

The quite different actions called for in these two situations where precisely the same quantitative data are observed, emphasise the need for flexibility and examining the context in the planning and mainstreaming processes, as well as the necessity for detailed information and data analysis.

Even in a single setting, available data are often differently interpreted, which can create problems in terms of policy direction. Barbara Bailey (1997) presents quantitative data on education in the Caribbean, which show the obvious gap in favour of females in literacy at both secondary and tertiary levels of education in the region. This and similar quantitative data have been used by Miller (1994) to justify a male marginalisation thesis, and have led to calls for an examination of male under-achievement in education in the Caribbean. Lindsay (1997) challenges this on the basis of the author's reliance on quantitative data and a narrowly focused methodological approach. She deplores the lack of in-depth investigation and analysis, which would bring to light deeper underlying issues. Bailey, discussing the data she presents, which have been used in support of the male under-achievement lobby, notes that:

"These data have been taken as an indication that equality of educational opportunity for women is not an issue in the Caribbean and that women are the privileged group in this respect. Little attention is being given to the fact that in spite of this supposed privilege, women in the region ultimately are at a greater disadvantage in the market-place and in the home. The gender gap in favour of females at the tertiary level merely indicates that men need lower levels of education than women do to enter the labour market. A study conducted by the UN Economic Commission for Latin America and the Caribbean (UNECLAC) and the United Nations Development Fund for Women (UNIFEM) in 1995 found that women need to have 4 more years of schooling in order to compete for salaries similar to those of men. This has been confirmed by World Bank studies which show that even though women in Latin America and the Caribbean enjoy equal opportunity for education as men, women generally are paid less even when they have the same education and length of work experience."

Bailey, 1997: 22

Figure 1   **Using Quantitative and Qualitative Data in Policy-Making**

Quantitative Data	Qualitative Data
More boys than girls do science and mathematics at secondary and tertiary levels. This gender difference is significant.	Science options are offered at the same time as home economics and office procedures. Girls are channelled into the latter options.
	Science texts refer to scientists in masculine terms, and do not feature women as scientists.
	Mathematical problems are usually framed in terms of 'masculine' activities.
	Most science teachers are men.
	In science classrooms, male teachers rarely interact with female students, and such interaction as occurs is usually demotivating for the girls. Boys have a similar experience in home economics and office procedures classes where the teachers are predominantly female.

Source: Leo-Rhynie,1996

The Policy Statement

Using the results of the gender analysis, a policy statement should be formulated in consultation with a wide range of stakeholders. The statement should be made the subject of community meetings, board meetings, staff and student meetings, home-school association meetings, past students associations meetings. It is through this discussion that the priorities for particular

Recommendations	Policy
Subject options should be available to both male and female students; where choices are offered these should not reflect sex stereotypes.	Male and female students should have equal access to all subjects in the curriculum. Within five years, the number of girls doing science at secondary and tertiary level should double.
Examples of female scientists should be identified and deliberately introduced in class discussions. Attempts should be made to develop equivalent mathematical problems using 'non-masculine' examples.	Detailed textbook analysis and review should be undertaken, with a view to developing and bringing into use, within five years, texts which are gender-sensitive, and which do not retain old gender stereotypes.
Attempts should be made to employ more female science teachers.	More women should be encouraged to become science teachers. The number of female science teachers should double in five years.
Gender awareness training must be provided in teacher training colleges as well among practising teachers.	Within three years, all teacher education institutions must integrate gender issues into their courses and ensure that graduates are knowledgeable about gender issues, how these operate and affect the learning process. Practising teachers must participate in summer programmes designed to increase their awareness of these issues and their effects. This should be accomplished in five years.

communities and institutions should be agreed. One approach would be to send a letter to all schools, universities and training institutions referring to the problems outlined above and policy options to address them, and to request students, staff and other workers to discuss these policy guidelines and make proposals on how to implement them.

Figure 2   **Examples of Two Different Situations with the Same Quantitative**

Country A		
Quantitative Data	**Qualitative Data**	**Policy Priority**
Ratio of girls to boys at secondary school increased from 1:3 to 1:1 over the previous five years	Perception by boys that school is not relevant to their adult lives, and their plans for the future	Examination of the curriculum to assess its usefulness/relevance to the male student population and revision where indicated
	Boys not attending school in order to work and earn in the informal sector	Determining how to encourage boys to attend school: ✦ legislative solution ✦ media awareness programme ✦ positive male role models
	Girls interested in school, encouraged by mothers to qualify themselves. Teenage pregnancy rate down.	Strengthen the initiative and encourage more young women t attend school. Increase family planning services.

Source: Leo-Rhynie, 1996

The policy document must be explicit in terms of what is required and the system must be supportive of those requirements. Where a top-down strategy is employed, establishing a policy environment in which gender is taken into account should be a priority objective. A policy document which emanates from an environment that is not gender-aware and gender-sensitive, but merely seeks to fulfil external requirements, may have little effect. The decision-making hierarchy of the Ministry of Education, for example, should reflect the numerical gender balance required of School Boards and institutional staff complements.

Policy documents emanating from Ministries of Education ought to:
✦ be clear;
✦ state goals which are desirable at a national level;
✦ include a timeframe for achievement of these goals so that progress can be measured;

untry B		
antitative Data	**Qualitative Data**	**Policy Priority**
tio of girls to boys at secondary ool increased from 1:3 to 1:1 er the previous five years.	Increase in school building pro-gramme over the past five years has created more secondary school places, especially for girls	School building programme to continue with emphasis on places for both girls and boys
	Media programmes encouraged parents to allow their daughters to complete secondary education	Media programmes to continue
	Great interest shown by both girls and boys in completing secondary schooling and accessing tertiary level education	Devise strategies to maintain the level of interest and build motivation

✦ focus on the more strategic and long-term gender needs of the system. The short term, practical needs can usually be met through operational objectives set at the local level; and
✦ include enforceable proposals where legislation is involved. For example, where compulsory attendance is legislated for girls as well as boys to age 16, create mechanisms to ensure that this is monitored and that there are sanctions for non-compliance.

Resource Allocation

The Ministry of Education should also have the resources to implement those recommendations and policies that are national in scope. So, for example, when there is a requirement that the curriculum of the teachers' colleges include a gender focus within a three-year time span (policy statement), the resources need to be available to prepare the teacher educators to develop their knowledge in this area, to carry out the necessary curriculum review and to integrate gender in their programmes of study (institutional objectives).

The fair and equitable allocation of the benefits of education is influenced by a focus on other major areas of concern, such as issues of quality and relevance, declining financial resources, the reduction in the status of the teaching profession, the perceived fall in educational standards, the speed with which technological change is taking place, and the importance of new technology in development. In many Commonwealth countries, these concerns have to be addressed in a context of significantly reduced resources (Sangster, 1994: 205).

It is important, however, that the allocation of these resources does not benefit one group to the detriment of others. Where resources for education are limited, considerations of gender in education policy and planning should be made a priority, so that resource allocation can be equitably made. Cultural factors, which can exert a critical influence on the involvement of females and males in the education process, should also be considered and addressed.

Policy Framework and Action Points

There follow a number of action points which governments may wish to adapt to suit their national circumstances:

School management, teachers and school staff

+ organise gender training/planning workshops for teaching staff, in co-operation with school management, parents associations and teachers unions, in order to provide school staff with an understanding of the construction of gender;
+ develop binding guidelines and disseminate them to all educational and training institutions;
+ publish a newsletter containing information and data on gender and education;
+ establish, for all staff, selection and promotion criteria that include specific expectations in relation to the achievement of gender equity;

✦ develop materials to assist teachers with assessment and evaluation procedures, including examples of assessment tools that consider the different experiences, interests and aptitudes of girls;

✦ encourage teachers to change their practice in a particular way, through, for example, promotion or allocation of resources; and

✦ ask schools to submit a plan of action to achieve gender equality and equity, and an annual report on progress made in this respect.

School organisation and practice

✦ ensure that the school dress code enables girls to engage in sport and active play;

✦ establish staffing procedures to ensure that women are represented in leadership positions;

✦ ensure that the timetable provides girls with real flexibility in their subject choice; and

✦ provide for the physical needs of each girl in relation to privacy, hygiene and clothing.

Curriculum

✦ ensure that gender considerations are included in all educational and training curricula, thus providing a curriculum which in content, language and methodology meets the educational needs and entitlements of girls and which recognises the contributions of women to society and values female knowledge and experience;

✦ include in the curriculum a range of teaching methods which best promote the active participation of girls in learning;

✦ provide access for girls to all areas of the curriculum, and establish the skills and confidence necessary to utilise this access;

✦ in partnership with the school community, provide information on conception, contraception, pregnancy, childbirth, child rearing, parenting and relationships;

✦ develop a curriculum which critically examines the gender distribution of work in families, households and paid work, and the relative values attributed to these different kinds of work by society; and

✦ provide advice on subject choices to ensure that girls do not limit their training and employment opportunities by the patterns of their study.

Educational materials

✦ ensure that textbooks and tests are gender-sensitive as regards the language, images and examples used therein.

Career counselling and guidance

✦ sensitise people engaged in career counselling on gender issues, thus ensuring that they also direct women to sex-atypical occupations;

✦ disseminate information to students and parents about career counselling and vocational guidance;

✦ devise a career guidance programme to encourage bright girls to further their education in areas where they are traditionally under-represented, e.g. technical and scientific areas; and

✦ guide boys and men also into 'female' occupations, which could eliminate gender segregation in jobs.

Girls' perceptions and attitudes

✦ stimulate girls to plan on working careers by changing their expected time allocations to both the labour force and home and their own perceptions of their roles and capabilities;

✦ establish mechanisms for identifying, supporting and monitoring girls at risk; and

✦ provide programmes for school teachers, counsellors and parents in order to enable them to understand those issues which place girls at the risk of not completing their education, issues such as income support, housing and childcare.

Parents' attitudes and involvement

✦ set up parent-teacher organisations to increase parental awareness of the benefits of educating and training girls and to involve parents more with schooling in general; and

✦ engage parents and the community in the development of programmes and materials that enhance and develop awareness of the impacts of gender construction.

Employers' attitudes

✦ induce employers to change their attitudes and practices as regards the perceived roles of women, e.g. by requiring that contractors tendering for government contracts do not discriminate on the basis of gender and ensure non-discriminatory treatment in recruitment, training and upgrading of minorities, or by threatening to enforce action by government agencies on the basis of anti-discrimination legislation.

Sex education

+ give advice to young girls and boys on avoiding unwanted pregnancies and on reproductive health, HIV/AIDS and other sexually transmitted diseases.

Sex-based harassment

+ develop programmes that teach girls and boys effective communication and conflict resolution skills;
+ develop policies at school level to demonstrate that sex-based harassment is unacceptable behaviour and ensure that it is punished; and
+ provide programmes and materials that inform school and wider communities about the underlying causes of sex-based harassment and its impact on the education of girls.

Vocational training

+ prohibit discrimination in vocational education and apprenticeship programmes;
+ take affirmative action to recruit more women to vocational education and apprenticeships;
+ ensure that girls are familiarised with vocational education and apprenticeships, set up orientation programmes and provide connections with potential employers; and
+ require government contractors to provide on-the-job training opportunities for women or to participate in training programmes that include women and minorities.

Affirmative action

+ put in place a programme to give preference to women in terms of education and training and career advancement until such time as women are available in sufficient numbers and at sufficiently high levels to ensure fair competition.

Image of women

✦ devise strategies to project a more positive image of women's working abilities and promote their entry into non-traditional occupations. Non-governmental organisations can play an important role in reorienting society's and men's attitudes to acceptance of new employment roles for women.

References

Bailey, B (1997). "Not an Open Book: Gender Achievement and Education in the Caribbean." In Mohammed, P (ed.) Working Paper No. 1, Centre for Gender and Development Studies: University of the West Indies.

Bellew, R T and King, E M (1993). "Educating Women: Lessons from Experience." In King, E M and Hill, M (eds.). *Women's Education in Developing Countries: Barriers, Benefits and Policies.* Baltimore: published for the World Bank – Johns Hopkins University Press.

Boserup, E (1970). *Woman's Role in Economic Development.* New York: St. Martin's Press.

Commonwealth Secretariat (1990). *Eleventh Conference of Commonwealth Education Ministers' Report.* 29 October – 2 November. London.

Commonwealth Secretariat (1994). *Twelfth Conference of Commonwealth Education Ministers' Report.* 27 November – 1 December. London.

Commonwealth Secretariat (1995). *The 1995 Commonwealth Plan of Action on Gender and Development: A Commonwealth Vision Agreed in Principle.*

Gore, J and Luke, C (eds.) (1992). *Feminism and Critical Pedagogy.* New York/London: Routledge.

Jahan, R (1995). *The Elusive Agenda: Mainstreaming Women in Development.* Dhaka: University Press Ltd and London and New Jersey: Zed Books.

Leo-Rhynie, E (1996). "Gender Issues in Education and the Implications for Labour Force Participation". In Hart, K (ed.). *Women and the Sexual Division of Labour in the Caribbean.* 2nd edition. Jamaica: Canoe Press.

Lindsay, K (1997). "Caribbean Male: Endangered Species?" In Mohammed, P (ed.). Working Paper No. 1, Centre for Gender and Development Studies: University of the West Indies.

Longwe, S H and Clarke, R (1994). *Women in Development, Culture and Youth: Workshop Preparatory Readings 1 – 3.* Lusaka, Zambia: Longwe Clarke and Associates.

Massiah, J (ed.) (1993). *Women in Developing Economies: Making Visible the Invisible.* Oxford: Berg Publishers and Paris: UNESCO.

Measor, L and Sikes, P (1992). *Gender and Schools*. London: Cassell.

Miller, E (1994). *Marginalisation of the Black Male*. 2nd edition. Jamaica: Canoe Press.

Molyneux, M (1985). "Mobilisation Without Emancipation? Women's Interests, State and Revolution in Nicaragua." *Feminist Studies*, 11, 2.

Moser, C (1989). "Gender Planning in the Third World: Meeting Practical and Strategic Needs". *World Development*, 17, 11.

Ostergaard, L (ed.) (1992). *Gender and Development: A Practical Guide*. London/New York: Routledge.

Overholt, C; Anderson, M; Cloud, K and Austin, J (1985). "Women in Development: A Framework for Project Analysis". In Overholt, C et al (eds.). *Gender Roles in Development Projects*. Connecticut: Kumarian Press.

Roopnarine, J L and Mounts, N S (1987). "Current Theoretical Issues in Sex Roles and Sex Typing". In Carter, D B (ed.). *Current Conceptions of Sex Roles and Sex Typing: Theory and Research*. New York: Praeger.

Sangster, A (1994). "Education and Training: Key Elements in the Development Process". In Lewis, P (ed.). *Jamaica: Preparing for the Twenty-First Century*. Jamaica: Ian Randle Publishers.

United Nations (1995). *Beijing Declaration of the Fourth World Conference on Women*.

UNDP (1995). *Human Development Report 1995*. New York: United Nations Development Programme.

UNICEF (1995). *The State of the World's Children*. New York: United Nations Children's Fund.

World Bank (1996). *Implementing the World Bank's Gender Policies*. Progress Report No.1. Washington, D.C.